CHEERLEADING
is for me

CHEERLEADING
is for me

Jim W. Hawkins

photographs by
Linda K. Vittor

Lerner Publications Company   Minneapolis

The author wishes to thank Brook Cantwell and her family as well as the many Pop Warner and other California cheerleaders who appear in the book. He also thanks Kim Rayburn, Jeanne Del Morale, and the other coaches, and everyone else who provided their moral support, including his family.

Photographs on pages 6 (left, top and bottom), 43, 44, 45 (top right) by Alan Oddie. Photographs on page 15 (bottom left) and 17 (right) by William Bible.

To my family and to the many cheerleaders I have worked with through the years

LIBRARY OF CONGRESS CATALOGING IN PUBLICATION DATA

Hawkins, Jim W.
    Cheerleading is for me.

    (Sports for me books)
    SUMMARY: A girl describes the gymnastics, stunts, motions, and other techniques her cheerleading squad uses.

    1. Cheerleading—Juvenile literature. [1. Cheerleading] I. Vittor, Linda K. II. Title. III. Series.

LB3635.H38   371.8′9   81-3719
ISBN 0-8225-1127-4   AACR2

Manufactured in the United States of America

International Standard Book Number: 0-8225-1127-4
Library of Congress Catalog Card Number: 81-3719

1 2 3 4 5 6 7 8 9 10 90 89 88 87 86 85 84 83 82 81

Hi! My name is Brook, and my favorite
sport is cheerleading. There are many skills
involved in becoming a good cheerleader.
I'd like to tell you about these skills and
about how I discovered the sport.

5

One day I went to a high school football game. My brother was playing on the team, so it was fun to watch them win. But it was even more exciting to watch the cheerleaders.

The minute I saw them, I knew that cheerleading was for me. The schools had both girl and boy cheerleaders. All of them had so much pep and spirit! They got the fans to cheer and support their teams. I had fun clapping and yelling with them.

I decided that I wanted to become a cheerleader the next time my school had **tryouts**. At the tryouts, those who performed the best would be selected for the cheerleading team. A cheerleading team is also called a **squad**.

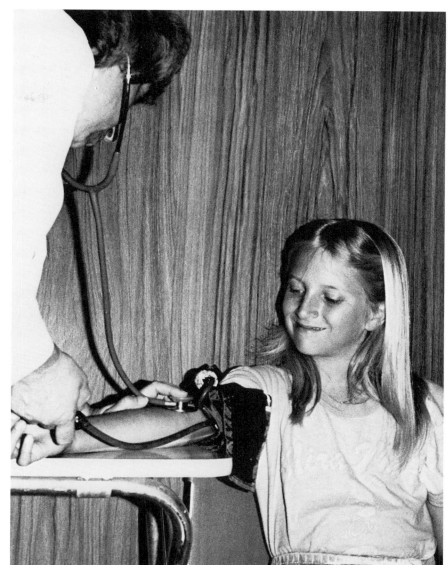

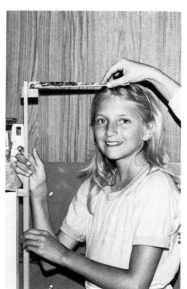

The announcement for the tryouts said that our parents had to sign a paper giving us permission to try out. We also had to get a medical checkup before we could go to the first tryout practice. I went for a checkup, and my doctor said I was healthy.

The first practice was held after school. Many returning cheerleaders joined us. The practice was run by the cheerleading coaches, Ms. Martin and Mr. Adams.

Mr. Adams began the practice with a long warm-up. He said that a warm-up was necessary in order to prevent muscle pulls, sprains, and other injuries. We warmed up with stretching exercises.

After we were warmed up, Ms. Martin explained how the new cheerleaders would be selected. Each one of us would be judged in four skill areas—a group cheer, an individual cheer, some gymnastics moves, and some jumps. The persons with the highest scores would make the squad.

Next we learned our first **cheer**. A cheer is made up of short, peppy words and arm and leg movements. The words to our first cheer were:

V-I-C-T-O-R-Y
Victory!
Victory!
That's our cry!

Your hand and arm movements are very important when you cheer, and they should follow the words. If you say "Fire up," for example, you will want to thrust your arm up in the air. Even your finger movements are important. **Blades** are hands with fingers together. They emphasize pauses and words like "stop." **Spread fingers** are used when you want to show excitement.

DAGGERS

CANDLESTICKS

Daggers are fists held straight out as if you are carrying a knife. You'll use daggers before moving your arms forward or together.

Fists held upright are called **candlesticks**. When you do this, you'll look like you're carrying invisible candles. You'll often use candlesticks before an upward arm movement.

Good arm positions can make your jumps look good, too. The arms will also give you lift. We would be scored on both the height and the style of our jumps. Holding your body still at the peak of your jump will improve your style.

One of the jumps we learned was the **Herkie.** It is named after L. R. Herkimer, who was the first cheerleader to use it. For this jump, keep one leg bent back and the other leg extended in front. Remember to keep your toes pointed.

We also did a jump called the **banana**. It has this name because you hold your body in the curved shape of a banana. Arms and legs are extended. The **C-jump** is done in much the same way.

BANANA

C-JUMP

When jumping or cheering as a group, you must try to always move together. The secret to moving together is starting off together. Our group used a signal. Our signal to begin was when the leader said, "Ready, hit it!" To end together, we all froze in an identical pose for a few moments.

Cheerleaders also have to do gymnastics moves. At the tryouts, we would be judged on a **cartwheel,** a **round-off,** and the **splits.** I practiced hard until I could do the cartwheel and the round-off in a perfectly straight line.

CARTWHEEL

ROUND-OFF

Cartwheels and round-offs begin in the same way. But the landings are different. When doing a cartwheel, you land one foot at a time. When doing a round-off, you snap your legs together in midair, make a quarter turn with your hips, and land with your feet together, facing the opposite direction.

Splits are an exciting way to end a cheer. To do the splits, slide one leg back on the inside of your foot. Slide your other leg forward, and keep your heel flat. Don't bounce, as this could cause a muscle injury.

You may not be able to go down to the floor on your first try. But if you practice every day, splits will become easier to do.

I practiced all of the cheers, jumps, and gymnastics moves that our coaches taught us. It helped to practice at home in front of a mirror. Soon I had memorized all of the words and moves. Still, I was nervous on the day of tryouts.

Ms. Martin gave a short talk before the tryouts began. She said that the judges would be watching to see how well we performed the basic moves. They would also look at how fit we were and how much pep we had. After all, cheerleaders must be able to keep active for long periods of time.

Soon it was my turn to try out. Even though I was nervous, I remembered to smile and show spirit. I also remembered to look at the audience. I made one small mistake, but I recovered quickly and kept on going.

After the tryouts, Mr. Adams announced the new cheerleading team. I had made the squad! I felt really good.

Right away we began to organize the squad. One of our first duties was to select our uniforms. The catalogs were filled with many different styles for boys and girls, so it was a hard decision. We finally picked blue and gold uniforms because they were our school colors.

We knew we would need a lot of coaching and practice. So the new squad and our coaches enrolled in a five-day cheerleading camp. Many squads from all over the state were there. We slept overnight in dormitories. It was fun making new friends and exchanging ideas about cheerleading. But we worked hard, too.

One of the things we learned at camp was how to improve our voices for cheering. You can lose your voice if you cheer from your throat. It is better to cheer from your **diaphragm.** The diaphragm is a muscle between your chest and your stomach. If you put your fingers in both places and cheer loudly, you can feel the difference cheering from your diaphragm makes.

Running will help to build the lung power you'll need for loud and strong cheering. And some cheerleaders use a **megaphone** to sound even louder. A megaphone is a cone-shaped device that points your voice in one direction.

The camp instructors also showed us some tips on using **pompons** in our cheers. Pompons are big balls of paper or plastic. You can do punches and claps with them. They help to emphasize words in a cheer, and they look very bright and colorful.

You can use pompons for **spell outs,** too. This is when your squad forms letters with the poms. For instance, you might want to make the initials of your team's name. Since several cheerleaders must work together, the spell outs should be practiced carefully so there aren't any gaps between the letters.

The **explosion** is another great pompon movement. It is an exciting way to end a cheer. For the explosion, the cheerleaders thrust their pompons in different directions. You can also do a **star**. A star is like an explosion, except that the poms form a star shape.

STAR

EXPLOSION

Swaying pompons is a good way to build rhythm in your cheers. Rhythm is important so the fans can follow the cheer easily. If you are doing a cheer without pompons, you can keep time by clapping, snapping your fingers, or rocking your body.

You can also build rhythm by having your squad repeat a certain motion down a line. This is called **rotation**. Each person performs the move in turn. A variation is to have every *other* person perform the motion.

Keeping time is even more important when you put your moves to music. Doing moves to music is called **songleading**. You do gestures and motions to fit the words of a song. This kind of cheering is really fun, and the fans love to join in.

The instructors at the camp also taught us some **partner stunts**. These routines require two cheerleaders working together. **Shoulder sits** are the easiest for me. You just jump up, and your partner helps to lift you on to her shoulders. You can **dismount**, or come down, in several different ways.

Another partner stunt is the **huggie bear.** To do the huggie bear, you catch your partner in a forward cradle. The upper partner is wrapped around the lower one. Arms go around the neck.

While many stunts require only two people, **pyramids** are usually done with the whole squad. Pyramids are special formations and designs that are built with people's bodies. Some pyramids have three people and are really just triangles. Others are more difficult.

No talking is allowed during pyramid building. So you really have to be careful. You should have a **spotter** to help you. A spotter stands ready to brace someone who slips or starts to fall.

You'll also need steady **bases**. These are
the people on the bottom who support the
weight of the people on the next level. If
you are on top, you should put your weight
on the base people in one of three places
—the thigh, the small of the back, or the
base of the neck. The last step in building
a pyramid is positioning your arms and
hands. Keeping steady is very important!

On the last day of camp, we had a competition between squads. We were judged on style, spirit, timing, unity, jumps, arm positions, and more. Our squad won a trophy, which made us all very happy. But we were sad to say goodbye to our new friends.

Now our squad had its first football game to look forward to. The first game was coming up on Saturday. So we were in charge of the pep rally at school on Friday. A pep rally is a chance to show your school spirit and teach the crowd new cheers. Everyone at the pep rally got really fired up! This made the team members want to win more than ever.

We had planned ahead so that our pep rally would be the best ever. We made signs to greet the team. Some groups from the school put on **skits**, or short plays. They were really funny and put everyone in the mood for a great game.

The football game was very exciting.
We got to perform many of the cheers we
had practiced. Part of a cheerleader's job
is to know when to use certain cheers. You
must know the rules of the game in order
to choose the right cheer at the right time.

There are also times when you should not cheer. For example, you should not cheer when team signals are being called or when an opponent is injured. And you should be courteous and wait for the opposing fans to finish their cheer before you start your own.

Remember that cheerleading is a sport,
so you must show good sportsmanship.
The crowd is watching you and counting
on you to raise their spirits. So be a leader,
and cheer for your team. I'd love to see
you become a cheerleader, too!

Words about CHEERLEADING

BASE: In a stunt or pyramid, the people on the bottom who support the body weight of others

CAPTAIN: The person chosen to lead a cheerleading squad

CERTIFIED COACH: A specially trained sponsor who is a member of a national cheering association

CHANT: A songlike series of words, often with repeats, done at any time during a game

CHEER: A series of words and motions performed to motivate a crowd during breaks in a game

COMPETITION CHEER: A three- to five-minute cheer made up of several shorter cheers featuring special stunts

DIAPHRAGM: The part of the body below the chest cavity from which vocal power is pushed

GAME PLAN: The plan that states which cheers will be used during specific parts of a game

LIFT: To raise a partner's body off the ground

LUNGE: A full body movement in one direction

MAIN CONTROLLER: The cheerleader who signals to the squad and crowd how many times a chant will be done

MASCOT: A cheering squad member who is special in costume, age, or size

MEGAPHONE: A cone-shaped device used to point the voice in one direction

PEP RALLY: A program to develop fan spirit through cheers, skits, and speeches

RUN THROUGH: A large paper sign for the team members to burst through as they make their entrance at a pep rally or game

REPEATS: Chants in which the audience echoes back the same words used by the cheerleaders

SKIT: A short play, usually humorous

SPIRIT: Enthusiastic support

SQUAD: A team of cheerleaders supporting a certain team

THRUST: A quick extension of the arm in any direction

TRYOUT: A test of skills in which judges choose the best people for the cheerleading squad

YELL LEADER: A cheerleader who motivates the crowd through loud yells

ABOUT THE AUTHOR

JIM W. HAWKINS was involved in spiritleading during his elementary school days and at San Diego High. Today he is the chairman of the Committee for More School Spirit and coaches several cheerleading squads. He has helped with United Spirit Association and National Cheerleaders Association camps and is a founding member of the Dynamic Cheerleaders Association's Advisor's Association. A certified teacher, Mr. Hawkins also spends time working with other youth sports and doing freelance writing.

ABOUT THE PHOTOGRAPHER

LINDA K. VITTOR, who majored in journalism at San Diego State University, is the author/photographer of six published articles on do-it-yourself projects. She holds a pilot's license and recently helped to edit a book about flying. Ms. Vittor enjoys many sports, including horseback riding, skiing, and bowling, and her daughter, Jodie, was a Pop Warner football cheerleader.